A Biography by

Jack L. Roberts

SCHOLASTIC INC.

New York Toronto London Auckland Sydney
Mexico City New Delhi Hong Kong

Cover photo by

John Atashian/Retna Ltd.

Printed in the U.S.A.

ISBN 0-439-05698-5

1 2 3 4 5 6 7 8 9 10 23 06 05 04 03 02 01 00 99

Table of Contents

Babyface is the nickname for Kenny Edmonds. And that's a big name in music.

INTRODUCTION

The year is 1970. Eleven-year-old Kenny Edmonds is in love (again). So what does he do? He writes the girl a love song. There's only one problem. He is too shy to give it to her. So she never knows how he feels.

Fast forward to the present. Kenny Edmonds is still writing love songs. Now he is known as Babyface. (And, he says, he's still a little shy.)

He is also the buzz of the music industry. The best singers in the business want to work with him. They want him to write and produce their albums.

Take, for example, Boyz II Men. In 1992 Babyface wrote and produced a song for them. It was called "End of the Road."

The song is about a guy whose girlfriend wants to break up with him. They have come to the "End of the Road." The guy can't let her go. "*Girl, each time I try, I just break down and cry.*"

"End of the Road" became one of the biggest-selling singles of all time. It stayed number one on the *Billboard* Hot 100 chart for 13 weeks.

That's not bad for a shy kid from the Midwest. But his success does not surprise his family and friends. After all, Kenny always had big dreams.

Babyface has always written what he didn't have the nerve to say.

Always in Love 1

Kenny Edmonds was born on April 10, 1959, in Indianapolis, Indiana. He was the fifth of six sons. Kenny started writing love letters in kindergarten. "Puppy love hit me hard," he admits. Later, in junior high school, he would even write love letters for his friends.

But he could never tell girls he liked how he felt. So he wrote his feelings down in a diary. It was supposed to be secret.

One day, Kenny's brother Kevon found the diary. He read about Kenny's crush on a girl named Rhonda. Kevon wanted to do Kenny a favor. So he told Rhonda how Kenny felt about her. (That's some favor, right?)

Rhonda called Kenny. When Kenny heard

her voice, he froze. “All I could do was hang up,” he says. That was the end of the romance.

Why do you think that Babyface was more comfortable writing *about* girls than talking *to* them?

Kenny told himself that someday he'd have a hit. He'd just keep working until he did.

2 The Goal

When Kenny was in the eighth grade, his father died of lung cancer. Life was hard after that. But Kenny never felt poor. "We didn't have a lot of money. But we always had enough food and clean clothes," he says.

In junior high, Kenny started fooling around with the guitar. By the time he was in high school, he was hanging with local funk and top-40s bands. Some moms might have minded. Kenny's didn't. "Mom believed in me," he says.

In 1976, Kenny graduated from high school. For the next few years, he played guitar with different bands. They performed mostly in Holiday Inns or on Air Force bases.

From 1982 to 1987, Kenny kept writing

songs. He recorded his songs and tried to sell them to record producers. It was in a recording studio, in fact, that someone gave him the name Babyface.

But his songs still weren't getting any attention. "I had tons of songs that nobody would take," he says.

Those years were tough. Kenny must have wondered if he'd ever succeed. Still, he kept at it. "I never took vacations," he says. "It was all about getting a hit."

Finally, in 1987, Babyface got his big break. He produced a song for a group called the Whispers. The song, "Rock Steady," became a major hit. It went to number one on *Billboard*'s rhythm-and-blues chart.

Babyface was thrilled. At last he was a success. But that was only the beginning.

Babyface was on his way to the top. And he was working with a lot of stars on the way.

3 Top-Ten Hits

Suddenly, Babyface was hot. He was an unstoppable hit machine.

He wrote and produced hits for the biggest names in rhythm-and-blues and pop music. There was "The Lover in Me" for Sheena Easton. It went to number two on the pop charts. For Bobby Brown, there was "Every Little Step." Whitney Houston had a hit with "I'm Your Baby Tonight."

Babyface also wrote for himself. In 1989, he released his second solo CD. It was called *Tender Lover*. It soon sold more than two million copies and became "double platinum."

That same year, Babyface and his friend L.A. Reid formed a record company. They called it LaFace Records. They started to produce CDs. They helped singers decide what songs to record. They hired all the different people it takes to make a record.

Over the next few years, they produced 75 top-ten hits. They also started the careers of TLC and Toni Braxton.

Few people knew Toni until Babyface recorded a song with her. It was called "Give U My Heart." Later, Babyface wrote a song called "Breathe Again." It was a big hit.

In 1993, Babyface released his third CD. It was called *For the Cool in You*. The title song is—you guessed it—a love song. He sings to the woman he loves. He sings about "all the changes that I put you through."

The album became triple platinum.

Which do you think would be more exciting—to work with a big star, or to work with a new talent who you could help become a big star?

Babyface continued to work with superstars in the music industry.

4 Take a Bow

Stars kept asking to work with Babyface. One reporter said, "Everybody wants a piece of his broken heart."

In 1995, Babyface wrote a love song with Madonna. It was called "Take a Bow." It's about the pain of a failed romance.

"*I've always been in love with you. I guess you've always known it's true. You took my love for granted. Why, oh, why? The show is over. Say good-bye.*"

"Babyface is a hopeless romantic," says Madonna. "I adore him."

That same year, Babyface had a chance to do something new. He called it a "once-in-a-lifetime opportunity." He wrote or co-wrote most of the songs for a movie. It was called

Waiting to Exhale. The album stayed number one on the pop charts for five weeks.

In 1996, Babyface worked with Stevie Wonder. They wrote a song called "How Come? How Long?" It tells the story of a beautiful, smart girl. She falls in love with a man who hurts her. No one comes to help her.

"*How come? How long? It's not right. It's so wrong. Do we let it just go on? Turn our backs and carry on?*"

Even Mick Jagger said he wanted to do a project with Babyface. Jagger is the lead singer for the world famous band, the Rolling Stones. "That's pretty amazing for this little kid from Indianapolis," Babyface said.

Babyface had always been looking for love. He finally found it in a music video.

5 Love at Last

In 1991, Babyface was planning a music video. It was for his song "Whip Appeal." A beautiful young woman tried out for a part in the video. Her name was Tracey McQuarn. Soon, Babyface asked Tracey out.

"It was sparks at first date," Babyface remembers. By 1992, they were married. Four years later, in 1996, Tracey and Babyface had a baby boy. They named him Brandon.

Together, Tracey and Babyface formed a film company. It's called Edmonds Entertainment. The company produced its first movie in 1997. It was called *Soul Food*.

It was a simple but powerful story. It told how one young boy kept his family together in troubled times. *Soul Food* was a hit. Suddenly, Edmonds Entertainment was one of the hottest black film production companies in Hollywood.

BABYFACE PHOTO ALBUM

PHOTOS: SETH POPPEL YEARBOOK ARCHIVES

Babyface has been playing music since he was a kid. Here he is performing at a high school dance. His band was called Tarnished Silver. *Above*: His 1975 yearbook photo.

Babyface has worked with just about everyone. Here, he's with comedian Chris Rock. Listen for Babyface's name in the song "Basketball Jones" by Chris Rock and Barry White. It's from the movie *Space Jam*.

Babyface and Madonna at the American Music Awards. Together, they wrote and performed a song called "Take a Bow."

Babyface with Usher. On the right is producer Quincy Jones. He once said, "I envy Babyface a little. Everything he touches turns to gold."

Babyface with singer Whitney Houston. He wrote most of the songs in her movie *Waiting to Exhale.* The movie's album went to number one.

Babyface and Stevie Wonder. Stevie is one of the most successful singer/songwriters of all time. He and Babyface wrote a song called "How Come, How Long."

©STEVE GRANTIZ/RETNA LTD.

Babyface has won every music award under the sun. In 1996, he received 12 Grammy nominations for his work. That tied the 1983 record held by Michael Jackson.

©SONIA MOSKOWITZ/GLOBE PHOTOS

In 1997, Babyface won the Producer-of-the-Year Award. It was the third year in a row he won the award. He is shown here with singer Eric Clapton.

No matter how busy he is, Babyface always makes time for his family. Here he is with his wife, Tracey Edmunds. She runs a record company called Yab Yum Entertainment.

©ANDREA RENAULT/GLOBE PHOTOS

©FITZROY BARRETT/GLOBE PHOTOS

Babyface with his mother, Barbara Edmunds. After his father died, she supported the family. "Mom gave me the work ethic," Babyface says. "But she was cool about my music."

©NEAL PRESTON/RETNA LTD.

Babyface, Tracey, and their son, Brandon, live in a huge house in Los Angeles. It cost more than four million dollars!

Many people say that Babyface is a musical genius. But he says they're wrong. "I'm just a song man," he claims.

Babyface may be on the fast track. But his ego isn't.

A Good Guy

Babyface has written more than 100 top-ten hits. He has produced more than a dozen number-one hits. He is one of the biggest names in the music business.

Still, he is known in the business as a nice guy. He is honest. He is down-to-earth. He is a gentleman. His mother can be proud.

Most important, Babyface treats people with respect. "I've tried to lead my life without hurting anyone," he says. "I just try to be a good person."

Part of being a good person is helping with charities. In 1994, he starting speaking out about an important charity for babies. It's called the Boarder Baby Project. It helps thousands of unwanted babies.

And after the success of the movie *Soul Food*, Babyface and his wife gave $100,000 to the United Negro College Fund. He wanted to encourage kids to go to college.

Today, Babyface is one of the most successful people in the music business. A lot of guys might become stuck up. Babyface hasn't. He explains it this way:

"As a small boy, I played out my love fantasies by pressing a guitar to my heart and strumming little stories. I'm still doing that. It's just that today more people are listening."

What they are listening to are beautiful love songs. They are written by a guy who has always been in love with love. As Babyface explains, "Without love, there is no music, no songs, no stories worth singing about."

His fans would agree.

Do you think that stars like Babyface should help society?

BABYFACE'S AWARDS

1989: Wins BMI Pop Songwriter-of-the-Year Award (with L.A. Reid)

Wins BMI's Pop Music Award: Album of the Year (for *Tender Lover*)

1990: Wins BMI's Pop Songwriter-of-the-Year Award (with Janet Jackson)

1991: Wins BMI's Pop Songwriter-of-the-Year Award (with L. A. Reid)

1992: Wins Grammy Award for Best Rhythm-and-Blues Song (with L.A. Reid and Darryl Simonds, for Boyz II Men's "End of the Road")

Wins Grammy Award for Producer of the Year (with L. A. Reid)

1994: Wins Grammy Award for Album of

the Year (for *The Body Guard*)

Wins BMI's Pop Songwriter-of-the-Year Award

Wins BMI's Most Performed Song ("Breathe Again," recorded by Toni Braxton)

Wins *Billboard Magazine*'s Pop and Rhythm-and-Blues Songwriter-of-the-Year Award

1995: Wins Grammy Award for Best Rhythm-and-Blues Song

Wins Grammy Award for Producer of the Year

Wins BMI's Pop Songwriter-of-the-Year Award

Wins BMI's Most-Performed Song

Wins *Billboard*'s Pop and Rhythm-and-Blues Producer-of-the-Year Award

Wins *Billboard*'s Pop and Rhythm-and-Blues Songwriter-of-the-Year Award

Wins first American Music Award (AMA) for favorite Male Rhythm-and-Blues artist

1996: Wins Grammy Award for Producer of the Year (second year in a row)

Wins Grammy Award for Best Rhythm-and-Blues Song (Whitney Houston's "Exhale Shoop Shoop")

Wins Grammy Award for Record of the Year (Eric Clapton's "Change the World")

Wins National Academy of Recording Arts and Sciences Award for Producer of the Year

1997: Wins Grammy Award for Producer of the Year (third year in a row)

Wins National Academy of Recording Arts and Sciences Award for Producer of the Year

1998: Wins National Academy of Recording Arts and Sciences Award for Producer of the Year

Wins AMA for Favorite Soul, Rhythm-and-Blues Male Artist

Wins AMA for Favorite Pop-Rock Male Artist

Babyface's Albums

Babyface has released five of his own albums as a solo artist. Here's the countdown. . . .

1987: *Lovers*

1989: *Tender Lover*

1993: *For the Cool in You*

1996: *The Day*

1997: *MTV Unplugged*

Did you like this book?

Here are two other READ 180 Paperbacks that you might like to read.

The Band

It looks like Jake's band is about to get a big record deal. But is he about to ruin everything for everyone else?

Dina Anastasio

All in a Day's Work and Other Stories

Will Luisa keep her job? Will Mike get up the nerve to ask Valerie out? Find out in this book of short stories.

By Megan Stine, H. William Stine, G.E. Gaines, Steven Otfinoski, Alan Manning, and Virginia Schone

Glossary

charity	an organization that raises money to help people in need
exhale	to breathe out
opportunity	a chance to do something
platinum	a very valuable silvery-white metal. When used with albums, it refers to those albums that sell one million copies.
produce	When used with music, TV, and movies, it means to be in charge of making a CD, TV show, or movie.
released	When used with music and movies, it means made available to the public for the first time.
romantic	someone who enjoys romance
studio	a place where movies, television and radio shows, or recordings are made.
unstoppable	something or someone that cannot be stopped